Present and Emerging Threats to National Security in Digital and Cyber Space: An Analysis of Security and Legal Issues

Present and Emerging Threats to National Security in Digital and Cyber Space: An Analysis of Security and Legal Issues

Lieutenant Commander Bharat Singh (Retd)

Group Captain Raja Singh (Retd)

(Established 1870)

United Service Institution of India

New Delhi (India)

Vij Books
New Delhi (India)

Published by

Vij Books
(Publishers, Distributors & Importers)
4836/24, Ansari Road
Delhi – 110 002
Phones: 91-11-43596460
Mob: 98110 94883
e-mail: contact@vijpublishing.com
web : www.vijbooks.in

First Published in India in 2024

ISBN: 978-81-19438-87-7

Contents

Introduction

"Our movements and feelings are constantly monitored because surveillance is the business model of the digital age".

—Katherine Viner

Protection of Digital Assets by Armed Forces.

Owing to emerging technologies, the nature of warfighting is changing rapidly. Asymmetric warfare and low-intensity conflicts have been normalised. The nation-states continue to be in a 'No war no peace' state. At the time of war, the armed forces engaged in battle aim to inflict maximum damage on their adversaries. Apart from military capabilities, often the industrial-economic base of the adversary, which supports its direct warfighting capabilities, forms a legitimate target. More often than not, these industrial-economic assets are dual-role entities, contributing to both civilians as well as to a nation's military. The classification of industrial-economic assets as exclusively for civilian use or military for long has been difficult and sometimes not even feasible. During the recent terrorist attack on Israel by Palestinian terrorist organisation Hamas on 07 Oct 2023,[1] the Hamas fighters were found to be conducting operations from inside hospitals and in civilian locations.[2] Such scenarios give rise to complex contradictions in international laws and raise questions pertaining to violation of Laws of Armed Conflict and human rights by both sides. However, one who wins the information war in such a situation carries the day. Hence, the armed forces have to be geared up to wage and win an information war also, even in the thick of conventional battles.

It is also a primary responsibility of the armed forces to not only protect its military and strategic assets during the war but to also protect its national, industrial and economic assets, as they form the crucial backbone of its warfighting capabilities and support structure. The present domination of the Indian Ocean by the Indian Navy has ensured the safety of the sea-lines of communication or shipping routes for trade, and the offshore assets in both war and peace. Similarly, the deployment of available air-defence units near industrial bases during wars has always been done to protect them from enemy's air attacks. However, in the digital age, many aspects of industrial operations, financial transactions and management, governance and administration, the management of the economy and social interactions have largely shifted to digital platforms, thus completely changing the way how human society operates. This brings new vulnerabilities in wartimes and challenges for the armed forces; the final bastion where the buck stops. The defence forces are bound to be called to respond in defence of all national assets, including digital assets, whenever and wherever civilian institutions fail under enemy assault. The creation of the Cyber Command in the form of the Defence Cyber Agency, a tri-service organisation for cyber warfare roles, as part of the Integrated Defence Staff,[3] is a step in the right direction.

The transformation of the economy to a digital economy, shifting of the operation and management of economic and industrial assets to online digital platforms, along with the very high probability of interference by foreign powers and even by other cyber intermediaries, have created whole new scenarios and challenges for national security. The role of cyber-intermediaries and the sway their hold over Indian society needs to be thoroughly analysed. The armed forces will have to educate, transform and arm themselves with the ability and technical know-how to counter the emerging new challenges; including those on the distant horizon. It is therefore important that the nature of threats and challenges are properly discussed, understood, assessed and countered. It is also important that the existing related digital laws are understood in the right context by all security agencies involved.

CHAPTER - 1

Digitisation of Economy and Emerging Challenges

The Global Economy

The prolonged COVID-19 pandemic lockdown, the Ukraine-Russia war leading to imposition of severe sanctions upon Russia by the United States of America (US) and the European Union (EU), followed by cutbacks in supply of grains, oil and gas to the west by Russia in response has led to major disruptions in world trade routes and supply of grains, gas and petroleum. The associated steep rise in prices of oil and gas had resulted in considerable economic instability and recession in many nations across the globe. While in 2021, the Chinese economy grew at 10.6 per cent surpassing pre-pandemic highs to become a USD 15.66 tn economy by Dec 2021, from USD 14.5 tn in 2019. It seemed to have touched raw nerves in US whose' Gross Domestic Product (GDP) is estimated to have grown merely at 2 per cent, to a high of only USD 20.3 tn.[4] Many developed Western economies are facing serious economic challenges.[5] The United Kingdom (UK), a leading economy in Europe has seen a drop of 11 to 16 per cent in trade amounting to 12.6 bn Pounds owing to Brexit. The UK's trade with Russia has plummeted to historically low levels from Feb 2022 owing to the war in the region and subsequent sanctions, with imports of goods from Russia falling by 98.2 per cent; equivalent to 18 mn Pounds.[6] Germany, the industrial works horse of the European economy saw its annual growth rate dip to 1.9 per cent in 2022 from 2.1 per cent in 2021. The German economy is further likely to be adversely affected and witness contractions up to 0.7 per cent owing to the energy price surge, with inflation rising well over 7 per cent.[7]

Digitisation - the Saviour of Indian Economy in Recession

In spite of global economic downturns and uncertainties, the Indian economy acted like an oasis in the desert. India continues to be the favourite among investment destination, and has attracted USD 83.6 bn Gross Foreign Direct Investment (FDI) in financial year 2022. The PHD Chamber of Commerce and Industry, has projected that India is likely to attract FDI amounting to USD 100 bn in the years 2022-23.[8] The World Bank had reported India to be one of the fastest growing economies with annual GDP growth rate of 8.7 per cent in the year 2021. India is presently the fifth largest economy, having surpassed the UK and only next to the US, China, Japan and Germany in that order, and its economy is poised to touch USD 5 tn in the financial year 2025/26 and USD 7 tn by 2030.[9] The Indian economy has primarily been protected from the global economic recession owing to mass scale digitisation of services and the consequent upward movement of the masses towards digitisation. The digitisation of financial services, the low cost of digitisation and mobile connectivity led to the financial inclusivity of masses from the middle and rural classes in India, which earlier did not exist. Middle and rural classes of India now have access to a variety of services and sources of information. The sheer scale of the Indian population that got included in mainstream product and services generation gave the Indian economy an unparalleled boost and advantage. The scale of digital services provided by both public and private entities a necessary shield from the global economic recession. Pierrre Oliver Gourinchas, the Chief Economist of the International Monitory Fund stated:[10]

> "I think (digitisation) has allowed the (Indian) government to do things that would have been extremely difficult to do otherwise. Yes (it is a game changer). It is certainly something that is a very welcome development".

Now that the Indian government could reach the masses and distribute resources evenly, accounting and auditing became easy for government schemes. Checking the pilferage of funds and resources owing to corruption became possible. Both accountability and transparency improved. Digitisation changed the nature of the market and the buying patterns of people. With digitisation, the government could give targeted and pointed assistance where it was actually required and monitor leakage and pilferage. All these measures made the Indian economy more resilient, with the inherent ability to rebound in cases of global economic instability. It facilitated Government of India (GoI) in providing a wide range of services to its citizens.

Penetration of Digital Technology

The World Economic Forum (WEF), in its 2011 report[11] while assessing the impact of digitisation, stated that in South Asia alone, digitisation had an impact of USD 9.4 bn on GDP. The report further stated that digitisation is fundamentally reshaping business models, reducing entry and exit barriers and expanding the market reach in the Asian region. The corporates and businesses are increasingly relying on social media/digital search engines to advertise, explain and expand their business models, and to effect sales of products and services. As per the WEF's report on the Association of South East Nations,[12] Digital payment (e-banking and e-wallet) apps are the most widely used applications on social media/online transactions. Digitisation has assisted business entities in business expansion, expense payment, recognising and acquiring new customers, and dispute resolution. It has helped Micro Small and Medium Enterprises and Micro - businesses receive more loans from FinTech. The study found increased ease of transferring money to be the most significant benefit of digitisation.

As per the WEF insight report Aug 2022,[13] 95 per cent of the world's urban population and 71 per cent of the rural population have access to 4G mobile networks. Similarly, 72 per cent of the urban population and 37 per cent of the rural population have access to the internet and/or computer at home. The report emphasised that digital technologies have penetrated all domains of life, with people spending more than three hours every day on their smartphones. Smartphone users check their phones every 30 minutes. The digital technology is further being applied on building smart cities with smart homes, based on internet of things, based home automation technology, smart water supply, transportation through connected cars and public transport systems, health and emergency management networks, digitally monitored waste disposal systems, smart energy supply management, providing administration through digital services to citizens, security through digital identification, biometrics and digital signature etc.

Digital India Initiative

As a part of the GoI's Digital India Programme in 2015 large-scale digitalisation of public services was carried out. As per the report of the India Brand Equity Foundation (IBEF) of Apr 2022 India, a trust established by the Department of Commerce, Ministry of Commerce and Industry, GoI, as of Oct 2021, India had 1.18 bn subscribers of mobile phone services and 700 mn Internet users with 600 mn smartphones. Online banking was introduced by the Industrial Credit and Investment Corporation of India as far back as in 1996, thereafter in 1999, other banks such as HDFC, IndusInd and Citi bank launched electronic banking, and the trend continued marking the beginning of the 'Era of digital transaction' in India. The National Payment Corporation of India (NPCI) was formed by the Reserve Bank of India and the Indian Bank Association to create a robust online payment and receipt mechanism. Thereafter, the NPCI launched multiple technologies enabling digital payment like the Bharat Bill Payment System, Bharat interface for Money (BHIM), and the 'Cheque Transaction System'. Additionally, newer models of payment have been added to the list such as the 'Unified Payment Interface' which was developed by NPCI in 2016 to facilitate 'Peer-to-Peer', 'Person-to- Merchant Transaction'. Mobile wallet, a service that acted as a virtual wallet, wherein a payment card's information is stored on a mobile device, mobile banking, internet banking and so on.[14] As per the data provided by the Ministry of Electronics and Information Technology, total digital transactions in India at the end of the financial year and measured in Apr 2021, amounted to INR 15,887.88 cr in fiscal value, which rose to INR 24,832.68 cr in Apr 2022. Thus, it had increased at an annual rate of 56 per cent. Further, as per the Ministry of Electronics and Information Technology data, total BHIM UPI transactions in India in fiscal value, from Apr 2021 amounted to INR 4375.27 cr and rose to INR 9,230.26 cr in Apr 2022. Thus, it is increasing at an annual rate of 110 per cent. As per the report, published by IBEF during the financial year 2010-2011, a majority of the payments were made using paper currency. However, in the year 2019-2020 there was significant shift in the tilt towards digital/electronic methods.[15]

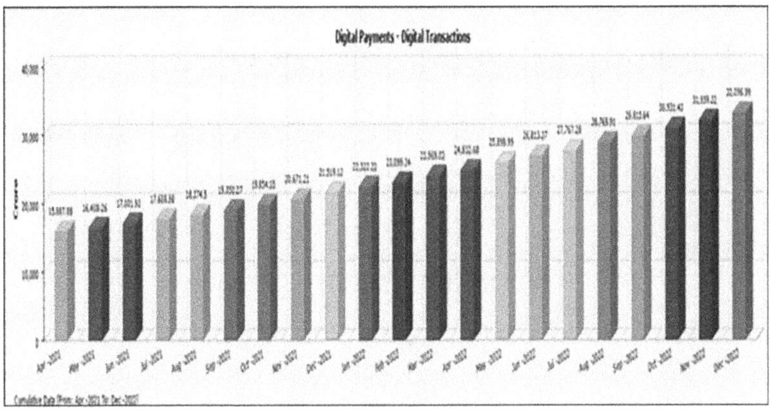

Figure 1.1. Bar Graph Depicting Total Digital Transaction in India w.e.f. Apr 2021 to Dec 2022[16]

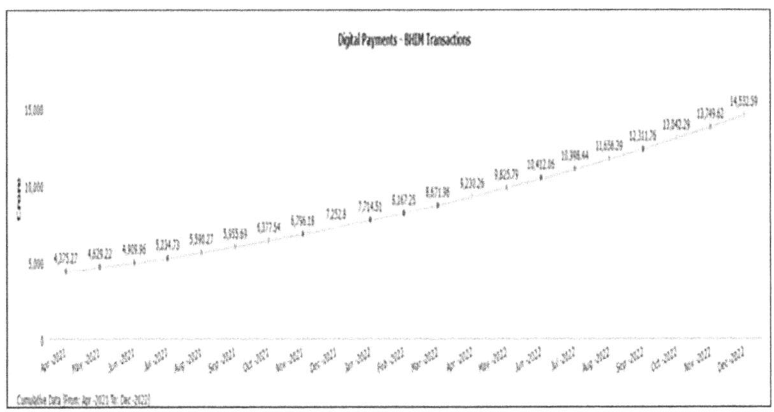

Figure. 1.2. Bar Graph Depicting Total BHIM UPI Transaction in India Between Apr 2021 to Dec 2022[17]

Chapter - 2

Digitisation of Citizen Data and Vulnerability to Information Warfare Through Social Media

Sensitive Data Generation with Use of Information Technology

With the use of Information Technology (IT) in governance, financial transactions, businesses and city administration, a large volume of data pertaining to cities and citizens is available online through cyber intermediaries, application and website operators. At present, data of more than 80 cities in the US and Canada is available in open-access portals. Similar is the case for various cities in east, central and south Asia, Latin America and the Middle East as well.[18] Many of these open-access sites and platforms give out the pulse of the city. The data provided could also be personal and sensitive in some cases. The data may pertain to a city or states' operating environment encompassing human life, traffic and choke points, city map, medical data, tax information, education, traffic, drainage, gas pipelines, electricity consumption etc. The real time data provided to dashboards assists in decision-making. The vast digital transactions are vulnerable to cyber-attacks. The digital transactions in the year 2010 to 2011 around the world amounted to USD 1.3 tn, whilst there was a surge in digital transactions in 2020 amounting to USD 45.9 tn around the world. The survey conducted by the WEF - Centre for Cybersecurity, of 120 cyber leaders in cyber security, brought crucial facts to light.[19] As per the survey, on an average, a company takes 280 days to identify and respond to a cyberattack. The threat actors are improving techniques and capabilities and making a shift towards multistage ransomware. The biggest threats to personal cybersecurity are ransomware, identity theft and the threat of critical infrastructure failure.

On 02 May 2021, two high-population density towns of the US, Los Angeles County in California, and Salt Lake County in Utah, suffered a distributed denial of service attack on the power grid. US government authorities have cited several countries, including China, Russia, and North Korea from where these attacks originated.[20] The attack caused interference in electrical system operations. Journal Utility Dive reported admission by Department of Energy secretary Jennifer Granholm to Cable News Network, a US media company, in Jun 2021 that US faces threats from its enemies who have the capability to shut down the US Power Grid.[21] India too faced a series of cyber and ransomware attacks on its civil infrastructure. In Sep 2019, India's Kundakulam nuclear power plant, under the Department of Atomic Energy, suffered a cyber-attack. It was detected to be 'Dtrack' from North Korea by cybersecurity firm Kaspersky.[22] In the Nov 2022, the five main servers of the All India Institute of Medical Sciences, New Delhi, suffered ransomware attacks. The initial investigation, after cracking the first layer of attack, pointed at hackers situated in China's Zhenan province and Hong Kong. The hackers were using a Virtual Private Network (VPN) to mask their IP Address. The hackers demanded INR 200 cr in crypto currency for releasing data of three crore patients. The attack affected the patient care services, which were subsequently shifted from online to manual mode.[23] The data included those of VVIP. The hackers were found selling the data on Dark Web. A similar attack occurred on 04 Dec 2022, at Safdarjung Hospital New Delhi. A firm named 'CloudSEK', which determines cyber threats, found data of 1.5 lakh patients of Sree Saran Medical Center being sold on the Dark Web and Telegram channels.

Applications by social intermediaries are being designed to be addictive. Excessive use of digital technology is also leading to severe digital addiction and behavioural disorders in citizens of various ages; the consequences of which are still unknown. Addictive digital content can affect a very large population segment and can be used to manipulate their ideas, behaviours and learning, which can have disastrous effects if done deliberately by foreign powers in control of digital intermediaries. As per Dr. Greenfield, digital addiction is as severe as gambling, and over 90 per cent Americans are in various stages of addiction. As per Dr. Greenfield every text, message or mail one gets activates the reward centre of the brain by release of bio-chemical such as Dopamine in the mind leading to addiction.[24]

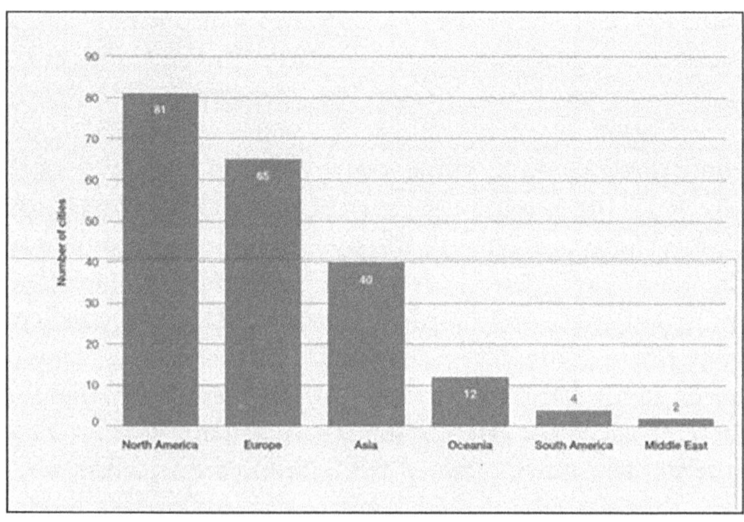

Figure 2.1. Number of Cities with Open Access Portals[25]

Social Media as a Tool for Spreading Disinformation, Social Disharmony and Political Destabilisation

Social media is a great enabler for socialising, meeting friends, airing one's own expression, civic discussion, news sharing etc. However, owing to its effectiveness in assuring human connectivity, it is now being used as a strategic tool for initiating political slugfests, distortions of facts and exercising stand-off social and political control through disinformation. As per the report from Freedom House, which conducted a study in 65 countries,[26] governments across the globe are deploying a variety of advanced tools to monitor internet users. In the survey conducted in 38 of the 65 countries, the political parties employed individuals to shape online opinions through the use of fraudulent accounts and hyper-partisan views. Large audiences with similar interest are targeted by circulation of inflammatory material. The cost involved is minimal. According to the survey, there are 3.8 bn people globally, who have access to the internet. Social media and cyber intermediaries have vastly enabled disinformation and disbursement of propaganda material during the election periods. As per the Freedom House report, there were increased online disinformation attacks in the US, both from domestic and foreign actors, during election period for political purposes and to undermine democratic processes. Social media and cyber intermediaries are also being used as tools for information warfare. It is further reported in the Freedom House report that both non-state and state actors were involved in distorting the media landscape by employing informational measures to manipulate elections in over 24 countries. The primary tools for information manipulation involved the use of bots i.e., automated accounts, hijacked social media accounts, fake news, paid news, propagandistic news, and paid commentators. The cyber-intermediaries are being used for the collection and surveillance of large amounts of data pertaining to citizens using advanced technologies including AI. The Freedom House research indicates that many foreign governments are acquiring data and using it to silence adversaries, perceived threats and silence undesirable expressions. According to a Freedom House report 71 per cent internet users live in countries where the government have arrested and imprisoned people for posting political, social or religious content. 65 per cent of internet users live in countries where attacks have been carried out and people killed for posting online content or their online activities. This has resulted in a sharp rise in global abuse of civil liberties.

Chapter - 3

Emerging Threats – New Technologies

Threat from AI, Social Media and Cyber Intermediaries Acquiring Citizens' Data

As per the report published by Ars Technica,[27] both iPhone and Android devices are constantly sending data which includes your phone's international mobile subscriber identity and international mobile equipment identity number, hardware serial number, Subscriber Identification Module serial number, local network details, media access control address of nearby devices, telemetry and location etc. The devices continue to collect information even when the phone is lying idle on an average every 4.5 minutes. An android device collects 20 times more data than iOS (Apple's mobile operating system) even when the user opts out of the collection of such information through the privacy settings of his device. As per the report, even pre-installed apps also made connections and sent data, even when they had not been accessed or used. As per the report an android device collected information from the search bars, YouTube, Google Docs, Chrome, Google Messenger, device clock etc., whereas iOS collected information from Siri, Safari and ICloud etc.[28]

The digitisation of organisations, corporations and economies, driven by the rapid development and adoption of technologies like blockchain, digital currency, digital documentation, digital signature, e-commerce and communication has increased the production of data exponentially and has also increased its relevance for the purpose of business intelligence and research for economic gains by businesses around the world. Data analytics has evolved into a separate field. An article published in the leading cyber security journal 'Cybersecurity Insiders' reported that Elon Musk, owner of Tesla and Chief Executive Officer (CEO) of SpaceX, is compelled to wipe out his data on his old phone and change the phone every 10 to 12 months owing to fears of someone getting access to his private data and to prevent information leak. The Journal claims to have obtained the information from Elon Musk's own admission made in a document submitted by him during one of the court hearings.[29]

Katie Holmes, in a website 'Ruler Analytics'[30] claims that marketers can track individual users from a website using Google Analytics, especially if they have a login authentication system on their website. In an online market place on the web, tools like Google Analytics help analyse what went into the mind of the purchaser before he actually made the purchase. This data can be used by cyber intermediaries like Google to reach new and existing customer bases through Google Merchandise stores. Apart from collecting data from websites touched by a Google account holder, Google Analytics can also collect behavioural data from a wide variety of systems such as, online point of sale system, customer relationship management system, mobile application, video game consoles and similarly placed other internet connected platforms that have its tracking codes embedded in them, and that get triggered every time a visitor visits or accesses them. The data collected from the above sources is used for compiling Google Analytics report for in-depth analysis.[31]The data is collected anonymously, and also comprises of a variety of details such as type of browser, language type, device type, Operating System (OS), traffic source etc.

Use of Artificial Intelligence

The new AI tools that can write stories and generate software code have the potential to disrupt traditional roles held by humans such as content writing, service enquiries, handling customers, copywriting, creating legal documents etc.[32] As AI models develops gradually and become smarter more and more, owing to automation, many of the current jobs are likely to be taken over by machines. Open AI's ChatGPT and Google's Bard, in the advanced stage of trial, are publicly launched freely accessible Generative AI, that can synthesise answers from large data set instead of just recognising patterns, and involve machine learning and feedback mechanisms for self-improvement. At the moment, YouTube is employing AI for removing violent content. The use of AI by business leaders has the potential to disrupt existing business models and ways of doing things including innovation and manufacturing. Presently, AI is un-regulated and has no governing mechanism. The present AI models have developed the ability to recognise patterns and objects in images, navigate maps, translate and transcribe languages, and recognise speech and emotions. They can write programs, do legal research, create logos, do painting, fly drones, undertake manufacturing, trade stock etc.[33] Their ability lies in executing action based on commands given, evaluating the successful outcome of tasks executed, providing feedback, identifying successful patterns from unsuccessful ones, and learning and improving. AI is able to repeat this cycle at a fast pace untiringly, surpassing human learning abilities. The ability is amplified by the ability to scan, assess and process a large number of databases in a short span of time. At present, only a few corporate leaders, tech giants have the ability to develop and run AI based systems. This gives them a phenomenal advantage over the have-nots.

The use of AI in genome sequencing, especially where the present human knowledge is primitive and insufficient has opened a new dimension in genetic engineering using AI. Presently, the capabilities of AI such as active learning, semi-supervised learning and Meta learning are being deployed along with gene-editing tools such as ribonucleic acid interface, zinc finger nucleaes, transcription activator-like effector nuclease and clustered regularly interspaced palindromic repeats with Cas9 protein is for genetic research.[34] This ability in the wrong hands has the capability to develop various virulent forms of pathogens which could be used as Bio-weapons, and to develop unethical engineered life forms beyond human comprehension.   Similarly, the technology in use of AI algorithms being deployed in the engineering of isotopes of elements and metals[35] has also the potential with appropriate modification and alteration to undertake research in the development of isotopes of radio-active material and hence the development of nuclear weapons or their models. The democratisation of a highly potent AI, especially in the hands of the wrong can have catastrophic consequences. This ability, if employed for creating weapons and disruptive technology, can fundamentally alter the balance of power in the world. 42 per cent of CEOs surveyed at the Yale CEO Summit expressed concern that AI can pose an existential threat to humans in the next 5 to 10 years.[36] AI, that is used to identify the cancer disease strain can be used to create genetically modified beings; AI trained to identify human emotions can be used to identify soldiers and kill them; AI used to control drones and deliver pesticides on farms, can be used to drop bombs or weapons of mass destruction. The use of AI for spying, surveillance and killing can have catastrophic consequences. AI can make it easier to develop weapons of mass destruction or create weapons that can kill on a large scale. The use of algorithm and data in AI can always be erroneous and cause AI to perform tasks erroneously.[37] Employment of an erroneous military application with lethal capabilities can have severe and irreparable consequences.

As per the Harvard economic professor Dr. David Yang, China has made tremendous progress in AI by importing AI technology from western nations.[38] As per Dr. Yang, weak democracies and autocratic regimes have a special interest in acquiring AI based technology for surveillance and monitoring. The Chinese history of the last 200 years including 400 Chinese emperors shows a quarter of them were assassinated by members of the government. The AI Index prepared by Stanford University that monitors the world-wide progress of AI has evaluated that China has made tremendous leaps in AI, and ranks among the top three nations attracting USD 17 bn in AI based startups alone, which is nearly one-fifth of global private investment. China is presently using AI in finance, retail and the development of advanced technologies.[39] The Chinese government agencies are using a wide array of AI technologies in monitoring their citizens both online and offline.

The Prime Minister (PM) of the UK, Mr. Rishi Sunak, hosted an AI Safety summit in Nov 2023 at Bletchley Park to understand the risks and rewards of using AI based systems[40], where many hypothetical scenarios of misuse of AI were discussed. SpaceX Chief Elon Musk, who was present at the summit shared his concerns about AI and advised that governments should exercise great caution in proceeding with AI based technologies. He advised that governments, in order to oversee issues pertaining to public safety would have to collaborate with corporates.[41] The PM emphasised that the AI could be used to develop and build chemical weapons and harm human interests, including promoting human trafficking, child pornography etc.[42] The emerging threats from AI based systems have compelled the US to launch its own AI Safety Institute. The US Secretary of Commerce Gina Raimondo, has expressed that she would want the US Safety Institute to form a formal partnership with the UK Safety Institute.[43] This may be an opportunity for India to develop its own AI Safety Institute and partner with top corporates and leading nations abroad, to learn early lessons. Early collaboration would help India to develop and set standards, and it would also expose it to the best practices around the world.

Quantum Computing

The use of AI and its efficient performance relies on the processing of enormous machine learning code and data that are fed into the learning loop. This requires the use of many variables and very high processing powers, especially when the work requires complex tasks, such as the study of sub-atomic particles and their behaviour. Quantum computers are elegant machines that using qubits (cue-bits), are capable of processing many variables and multi-dimension quantum algorithm. They are much smaller in size, possessing processing power far in excess to those as the best super-computers in class. They use super cooled super fluids to create super conductors so that the movement of electron is not faced with resistance.[44] Thus, where a traditional super computer reads binary 0s and 1s, a super cooled state quantum computer processor bypasses physical limits by superimposing 0s and 1s giving phenomenal computing abilities.

Google's 53-qubit sycamore processor in 2019 completed a task in 3.3 minutes that would take 2.5 days for a conventional super computer. In Oct 2021, the Chinese developed a 66-qubit Zuchonghi 2 quantum processor capable of completing the same task 1 mn times faster, leap frogging in the world of quantum computing.[45] The acquisition of such a technology by India's adversary should be a matter of great concern and a catalyst for an appropriate and parallel response by India to avoid getting left behind.

Social media giants like Facebook use advanced machine learning to serve content, recognise photos and target users with a variety of advertisements. Similar technologies are being employed by LinkedIn, Snapchat, Twitter, Instagram etc.[46] The advancement in AI like ChatGPT is being used to create content, software program, audio-visual content, mathematical calculation, essay writing etc. The tremendous automation capability offered by AI algorithms can have catastrophic consequences on employment and economics of a country like India, which has a labour intensive industry, including IT and the media sector. The nature of content and media created by AI by using a variety of software applications has the potential to create deep fakes, violate copywrite content, and create fake media content including fake voice, fake faces, fake videos that can disrupt the whole media industry, make actors and anchors jobless, violating their copyrights, which would have a bearing on society. According to Deloitte's 'State of AI in the Enterprise', Second Edition Oct 2022, 2018 survey, the executives, who very well understand the nuisances of AI and are considered early adopters, believe that the use of AI to create falsehood is the top of ethical risk that is posed by it.[47]

The threat of social media and cyber intermediaries, using the vast amount of data available with them along with behavioural analytics to affect the buying behaviour of consumers, and the market economy by manipulating the online search patterns of users is real. The Competition Commission of India (CCI) imposed an INR 1,337.76 cr penalty on Google for abusing their dominant position in the Android based mobile device ecosystem in multiple markets.[48] The CCI, vide its order highlighted the five markets areas Google was found to be abusing. The extract from the order of CCI highlighting the market abused by Google is reproduced below:

"……(a)   Market for licensable OS for smart mobile devices in India.

(b)   Market for app store for Android smart mobile OS in India.

(c)   Market for general web search services in India.

(d)   Market for non-OS specific mobile web browsers in India.

(e)   Market for online video hosting platform in India….."

The CCI found that, being a dominant player, Google could dictate to device makers to pre-install search applications, widgets and the Chrome browser which created entry barrier for competitors. Since all Original Equipment Manufacturers (OEMs) were tied to Google, other OEM could not sell other OS and search services. This restricted their access to open markets. Thus, Google could secure exclusivity for its search services and continued access to search queries which guaranteed and protected its advertisement revenues. For its competitors, the market seemed closed. Subsequently the CCI passed the directives to protect the Indian operating system market; the extract from the directives is reproduced below for reference:

"....(i)   OEMs shall not be restrained from (a) Choosing from amongst Google's proprietary applications to be preinstalled and should not be forced to pre-install a bouquet of applications and (b) Deciding the placement of pre-installed apps, on their smart devices.

(ii)   Licensing of the Play Store (including Google Play services) to OEMs shall not be linked with the requirement of pre-installing Google search services, Chrome browser, YouTube, Google Maps, Gmail or any other application of Google.

(iii)   Google shall not deny access to its Play Services Application programming interface to disadvantage OEMs, app developers and its existing or potential competitors. This would ensure the interoperability of apps between Android OS which complies with the compatibility requirement of Google and Android Forks. By virtue of this remedy, the app developers would be able to port their apps easily onto Android forks.

(iv)   Google shall not offer any monetary/other incentives to, or enter into any arrangement with, OEMs for ensuring exclusivity for its search services.

(v)   Google shall not impose anti-fragmentation obligations on OEMs, as presently being done under AFA/ACC (Anti-Fragmentation Agreement / Anti Compatibility Commitment Agreement) For devices that do not have Google's proprietary applications pre-installed, OEMs should be permitted to manufacture/ develop android forks based smart devices for themselves.

(vi)   Google shall not incentivise or otherwise obligate OEMs for not selling smart devices based on android forks.

(vii)   Google shall not restrict the un-installing of its pre-installed apps by its users.

(viii)   Google shall allow the users, during the initial device setup, to choose their default search engine for all search entry points. Users should have the flexibility to easily set as well as easily change the default settings on their devices, in minimum steps possible.

(ix)   Google shall allow the developers of app stores to distribute their app stores through the Play Store……"

Chapter - 4

Military Implications - Issues of National Data Privacy, Storage and Management

Data Sovereignty and Issues of National Security

The e-commerce and online communication technologies have resulted in national borders becoming irrelevant. Often, the data collected by social media organisations and cyber intermediaries is saved across various servers and cloud storage in trans-national locations. However, little is known about the policies of the cyber intermediaries and organisations dealing with sensitive information. Thus, the careless handling of information pertaining to the behavioural patterns of a large number of citizens, and citizens' data moving across borders can result in a serious security threat to national security of a country like India.

As per the report published in the journal 'The Expose',[49] USD 3.4 mn was paid to Twitter by the FBI to censor certain views and stories for political gains in America. As per the report, more than 100 former intelligence agents work in Facebook's content moderation department, agents are working on Twitter to keep check on the nature of content being circulated and to moderate the same. Further, the journal adds that Twitter worked in collaboration with US governments, especially, the US Department of Defence to promote and protect American propaganda and interest. American intelligence agencies used fake news, computerised deep-fake videos and bots to influence foreign governments. Quoting a video by investigative journalist Glenn Greenwald, 'The Expose' reports that the FBI, on a regular basis, seeks Twitter to release the location of Twitter users. It is highly probable, that similar activities would be happening against India.

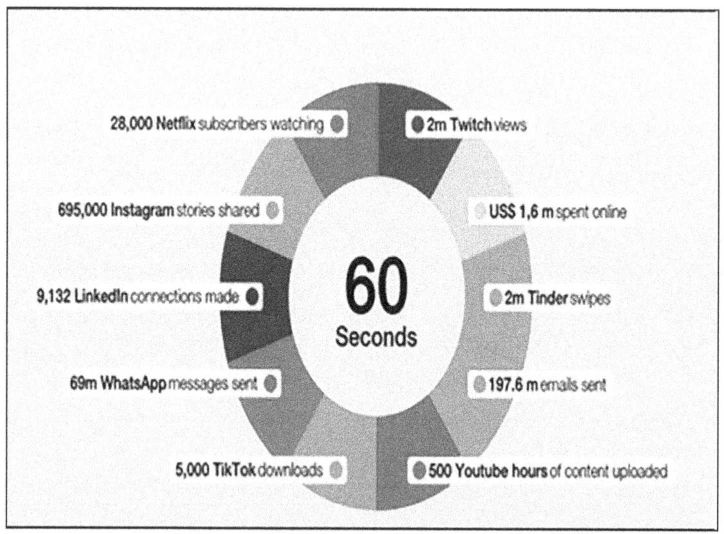

Fig 4.1. Estimated Data Created on the Internet in One Minute[50]

As per the Reuters, during the recent Ukraine-Russia war, the American government pressed Alphabet, the parent company of Google, Facebook and Twitter, to do more to curb news originating from Russian state-run media, and to demonetise their websites. The US companies were urged by the government to proactively suspend accounts involved in denying, glorifying or justifying aggression or war from the American perspective.[51] The Russian state run media Sputnik reported many of its sites to be non-functional with a bar imposed by YouTube on its channel. As most cyber intermediaries and social media giants have US origin, barring of news originating from Russia during the ongoing war allows US dominance in information warfare. It allows the US and its allied countries absolute dominance in the news landscape and one-sided capabilities of information warfare across the globe.

As per a report in the journal 'Task and Purpose,'[52] a Russian soldier gave away the position of himself and his unit when he shared pictures and videos of himself and his unit the 10th Spetsnaz Brigade on Russian social media VKontakte, equivalent to Facebook. Some of the photos shared by the Russian soldier had location tags, and were therefore easy to geolocate. The American intelligence shared the location information with Ukrainian forces with coordinates, which launched the attack and killed many soldiers. Task and Purpose further reported that in a similar case in the year 2020, a marine unit was killed during routine training exercise, when a soldier posted a selfie on the social media. A subsequent assessment showed the training area had a very high electronic signature as marines were constantly using phones. Similarly, on 27 Feb 2019, Indian Air Force aircrafts crossed the Line of Control and bombed the terrorist hideouts in Balakot, Pakistan, to avenge the terrorist bombing of Indian security forces in Pulwama, in the now Indian union territory of Jammu and Kashmir. The national technical research organisation, a technical wing of the Indian intelligence, used its surveillance system to identify 300 active mobile phones in the terrorist hideouts when the bombing was carried out [53] to calculate the terrorist killed in the aftermath of the bombing. These are apt examples of targeting based on precise location and identification facilitated by the detection of data transmission occurring from mobile apps and the use of IT devices.

Withdrawal of digital services by foreign organisations, on which citizen become dependent for their day-to-day lives can also have an adverse effect on the efficient functioning and stability of a nation, and make it vulnerable. A country like India should, as far as possible, rely on indigenous technologies for both hardware and software systems. This would require handholding and support from the government. Since the start of the Russia-Ukraine war, more than 400 technology companies have withdrawn from their operations in Russia. Qualquamm, a leading firm in the manufacturing of silicon processors, and US chipmaker Intel, stopped supplying their products and services to Russia. Google, an Alphabet owned company suspended YouTube, Google Play and other app-based services in Russia. It further stopped payments to Russian YouTube content creators. Russian apps of media outlets like RT TV network (a state funded international news television brand of TV-Novosti, formerly known as Russia Today) and Sputnik were removed from the Play Store. Apple has also disabled Maps, live traffic feature and other similar features from its devices and applications in Ukraine.[54] In his research paper titled "Strategic Buyouts Support Strategic Communication" Brig. Pawan Bhardwaj, YSM, a Research Fellow with the United Services Institute, New Delhi stated that effective strategic communication during the Russia - Ukraine war had become difficult with every one being a content creator, influencer or game changer. It was difficult to set a narrative and communicate with mases among the vast clutter of information. He further added the world's media is primarily controlled by six major media houses which control the entire media industry and exercise considerable influence. These include newspapers, National Amusement, Disney, TimeWarner, ComCast, News Corps and Sony running 24 hours, News channels, publishing houses and internet-based websites etc.[55] None of these major media houses have an Indian origin. Inferences can be drawn that there is a possibility that these media houses can become great assets in the hands of India's adversary as an effective tool for misinformation, and a cause of military discontent and political instability. The governments of these nations where these media houses are domiciled can arm twist or collaborate with them in activities harming India's interest in an adverse situation or in a situation of hybrid war. There is a view that in the battle of information warfare in Ukraine and Russia, hardly any media is airing Russia's perspective. A dominant US based private sector firm like Microsoft came to Ukraine's aid during the war and established dedicated secure lines for communication, to identify real time threats and offers technical support to them giving Ukrainians a technical advantage in communication.[56]

In an adverse situation like a war or emergency, foreign applications loaded with sensitive data about cities and citizens' private information can aid the adversary. The Russian troops were using Google Maps live traffic feature to target Ukrainian troops and monitor their movements. The Google live traffic feature would provide details such as areas facing traffic jams, high traffic, speed, road condition based on user data and movement. This could be used both by the Ukrainian and Russian Forces. Subsequently, Google disabled the live traffic feature of Google Maps.[57]

India too developed its own satellite-based navigation system 'Navigation with Indian Constellation' (NAVIC) after it found that the US had blocked access to GPS technology during the 1999 Kargil war. The NAVIC comprises of 7 to 8 satellites. S Ramakrishnan, Director of Vikram Sarabhai Space Centre, Thiruvananthapuram, had emphasised that in times of conflict some nations can deny critical services to us as a measure of arm twisting and hence we need to develop and rely on our own systems.[58]

CHAPTER - 5

Legal Provisions and The Role of Law Enforcement Agencies

Legal Perspective Encompassing Right to Privacy, Data-Localisation and National Security

An individual's privacy rights find their origin in natural laws and may have a direct bearing on the individual's survival. Guarding one's secret may be necessary to protect vulnerabilities and weak points from the adversary. The privacy of facts may be required for financial, economic or social success in the competitive world. Similarly, from a nation's point of view, its nuclear and military installations are a closely guarded secret. Any unauthorised publication or leaks of military, weapons and sensitive civil infrastructure, can endanger the existence of the entire nation, if it is obtained by state enemies. It can also lead to sabotage and the destruction of important assets by covert and spy operations.

The right to privacy in India is inherent in Article 21 of the Indian Constitution.[59] The Supreme Court of India has always liberally interpreted 'Right to life and liberty' granted under Article 21. The right to privacy is also recognised under Article 8 of the European Convention and Article 12 of the Universal Declaration of Human Rights to which India too is bound owing to Article 51 of the Directive Principle of State Policy of the Indian Constitution, under which India has an obligation to respect international law and treaty. In Kaushal Kishore V. State of UP[60] the Apex Court held that the fundamental rights can also be enforced against private individuals. Privacy rights, and the government's requirement for online surveillance therefore, have to be in sync and in balance with each other, with reasonable restrictions imposed on both.

Black's Law Dictionary has defined privacy as:

'right to be let alone; right to live without unwanted interference by the public matters with which public is not necessarily concerned; right of a person to be free from unwanted publicity.'

It goes without saying that privacy and personal liberty are two sides of the same coin, and one may be non-existent without the other. As per Justice Krishna Iyer ".... Personal liberty makes for the worth of human person...."

However, for the greater public good and security, the state often has to infringe upon an individual's right to privacy. In Kharak Singh V. State of UP,[61] the petitioner had challenged the provisions of secret and domiciliary visits under Uttar Pradesh Police Regulations. The petitioner, owing to his criminal past, was under surveillance. The surveillance was done to keep a watch on the petitioners' house which also involved visit to his house in the secrecy of the night. The petitioner challenged such provisions of the Uttar Pradesh Police Regulations. However, the Court refused to grant him any such relief in greater public interests, and refused to recognise any such right under the Indian Constitution.

In Govind Singh V. State of MP.[62] The Apex Court held that the right to privacy is a fundamental right subject to compelling state subject. The court defined the right to protect intimacies of home, marriage, family and motherhood. The court was against unrestricted state surveillance.

In People's Union for Civil Liberties v. Union of India[63] the Supreme Court delved into the issue of the right to privacy vis-à-vis telephone tapping by state authorities. The case highlighted the privacy of communication susceptible to abuse by tapping. It also recognised the legitimate requirement of state to tap communication for intelligence. The petitioner challenged the Section 5 (2) of the Indian Telegraph Act 1885, based on a CBI report that showed tapping of phones belonging to politicians, on directions of the government. The said section allowed officers of the central government and state government to intercept transmission of messages to maintain public order. As per the report, the CBI informed that Director Intelligence Bureau, Director General Narcotics Control Bureau, Revenue Intelligence, Central Economic Intelligence Bureau and Director Enforcement Directorate have been authorised by Central Government to intercept and tap phones. The Hon'ble court in the above said case recognised the right to privacy and laid down the guidelines for tapping of phones and deliberated that such powers should be exercised as little as possible.

Similarly, in M.P. Sharma V. Satish Chandra AIR 1954 SC 300 The registrar of the Joint Stock Companies, Delhi State, lodged a complaint against Messrs. Dalmia Jain Airways Ltd. with the Inspector General, Delhi Special Police establishment regarding an organised attempt to embezzle the funds of the company and declare a substantial loss, withholding true information from shareholders. Dalmia was the director and chairman of the company. On the basis of the FIR, the district magistrate ordered an investigation and issued a warrant which led to simultaneous searches in 34 places. Voluminous records were seized from various places owned by the petitioner and their privacy was violated. The petition under Article 226 claimed violation of privacy rights and fundamental rights under Articles 19(1)(f) and 20(3) citing many US judgements. The court rejected the claims and stated that reasonable restrictions on fundamental rights are permitted. The court further opined that seizure of documents, and search from premises is only for investigation and temporary and hence, cannot be held unconstitutional.

In Unique Identification Authority of India and Anr. v. Central Bureau of Investigation,[64] the Supreme Court passed an ad-interim order wherein it restrained the Unique Identification Authority of India from sharing biometric information of Aadhaar with any agency without the written consent of the person. The Central Bureau of Investigation had sought access to the huge database as an aid in investigating criminal offences.

The judgement in the Justice K.S. Puttaswamy V. Union of India[65] case is relevant to the present issue. Suspicion was raised when a vast amount of personal data was collected for the Aadhaar Unique Identification I-card. Questions pertaining to the right to privacy were raised with suspicion of the possibility of state sponsored surveillance. A retired judge of the Madras High Court Justice K.S. Puttaswamy, challenged the Aadhaar Scheme on the issue of legal validity. As per the petitioner, the scheme violated the right to privacy. The case was decided by a nine-judge bench. The Court held that right to privacy was limited by procedure established by law, but was similar to right to life and personal liberty. The Court noted that collection and possession of personal information gives immense power over an individual, and it could have chilling effect on exercise of dissent and on fundamental rights. The Court further held that invasion of privacy must be fair, for legitimate reason and reasonable. The Court further recognised the right to privacy and, intimacy irrespective of socio-economic status.

Limitation to Law Enforcement in Cybercrimes Cases

Quite often the law enforcement in the domain of cybercrimes is faced with multiple barriers as elaborated below:

- **Jurisdiction.** One of the primary barriers to the investigation of cybercrimes and law enforcement in cyber space is the issue of territorial jurisdiction. Often the cyber criminals are located remotely and outside the territorial boundary of the country, in a foreign nation. Thus, Indian agencies do not have territorial jurisdiction. The agencies cannot exercise a free hand in investigation and have to go through the route prescribed by international laws, which almost means that most cases will never ever get investigated or prosecuted owing to redtapism.

- **Statutory laws are Physical World Based.** For a crime to occur, the laws of the land or the rights of its citizens have to be violated. However, the laws have been drafted by the legislative bodies considering real world problems. Most laws have historical, cultural or a social perspective. The crimes in the virtual world, their consequences and damages cannot yet be fully anticipated or quantified properly by legislative bodies. The cyberspace and virtual reality are new phenomenon with real world implications. The digital world is constantly evolving and law enforcement agencies find it difficult to keep pace with them. There is rapid dynamism to it, which prevents the stability of concepts or ideas.

- **Difficulty in Detection and Hidden Identity.** The cyberspace allows the use of advance technology, VPN, dark web sites, encryption, remote operations and embedded technology to hide the identity of the true culprit. It is often difficult to detect and investigate crimes, and identify culprits. Often, investigating a cyber-crime may require a huge amount of technological resources, software and tools to undertake any kind of cyber forensics, and is beyond the capability of normal law enforcement agencies.

- **Technical Complexity and Rapid Advancement.** The rapid technological advancement in cyberspace outpaces law enforcement agencies pace of modernisation and adoption of new technology. The cyberspace criminals are mostly one step ahead.

- **Limitation of Law Enforcement Agencies.** The law enforcement agencies in India such as the police often grapple with issues like poor resources, infrastructure, technical training and equipment. Law enforcement being primarily a state subject, suffers from a lack of funds. State police, which often have jurisdiction within the territorial limits of the state face a herculean task and bureaucratic hurdle in prosecuting interstate or international criminals. Additionally, the absence of adequate laws governing wide ambit of human interaction, violation of rights and defining crimes in cyberspace require deliberation by Legislature.

Data-Localisation Measures Across the Globe

Many countries have taken measures to bar cross-border data flow by cyber intermediaries and software giants. Nations are making data localisation mandatory so that crucial citizen data does not move across borders. Data localisation requires companies to store and copy data locally. Recent laws in India may require processing data locally and taking sanction from the GoI before sending data across the border. The localisation of data also allows the government to monitor data and effect surveillance.

It is important that the difference between data residency, data sovereignty and Data localisation is understood, though on the ground, actual practices by cyber giants might blur the difference between the three. 'Data Residency' may be understood as the disclosure by an entity- business or government that their data is located at a certain geographical location of their choice. 'Data Sovereignty' on the other hand is a term that implies that the law of the land applies to where the data is stored, and is subject to protection and regulations of the domiciled state. 'Data Localisation' requires a copy of the data, including sensitive personal data is held within the boundaries of the state and is accessible by the government for law enforcement. This facilitates an audit of the data by a government without taking permission of any other government.

As per the journal information technology and innovation foundation[66], Argentina has prohibited the transfer of personal data to nations which do not have adequate data protection laws. The Transfer of data to a cloud storage location is also considered as international data transfer. However, international data transfer could be done with the express consent of the citizens. The journal reported that China has long been shielding its citizens from the import and export of unsanctioned information through the Golden Shield program run by its Ministry of Public Security. It is also popularly known as the 'Great Firewall of China'. The Firewall acts as a barrier which prevents citizens from accessing information and website critical to the Chinese Communist Party. However, in 2016 China implemented a series of data localisation policies. The China's new counter-terrorism policy requires all telecom operators, internet and telecom companies, who provide crucial telecom infrastructure relevant for national security to store citizen's data on servers located in China, and the Chinese government authorities will have access to encryption keys. In 2017, the Chinese government also issued a draft guideline which required extensive data localisation. Any movement of data across the border or offshore requires to undergo security assessment. Sending any out bound data transfer is prohibited if it causes a threat of any nature to the economic, political and scientific interest of the nation. In China, a popular social media platform 'WeChat' was widely monitored by administrators on the 30th anniversary of the Tiananmen Square massacre for any kind of deviant behaviour. The administrators remove tens and thousands of harmful contents on a quarterly basis.[67]

As per the reports of the Independent Journal, Russia has fined Twitter and Facebook 4 mn Roubles in Feb 2020, for going against the Russian Data Law and storing the data of citizens outside the national boundaries. As per the Russian law, social media sites and service providers are required to keep servers storing data of Russian citizens in Russia. Russia also fined Google and Facebook for failing to delete content found illegal as per Russian Laws.[68] In 2016, the Russian Government laid down extensive requirements for data localisation. The laid down regulations required that the actual content of the user to be stored for six months by the companies. Data included voice, text, media, pictures, sounds and video. Further the directives were issued to telecommunication companies to deny services to users who refuse to identify and cooperate with the government authorities or law enforcement agencies.[69]

The member states of the EU seem to be divided on the issue of data localisation policies. The European Commission intends to see the EU as one big digital market and removes barriers to data transfer and inhibitions regarding privacy. However, France and Germany, seems to be the biggest proponent of data localisation, primarily to maintain their digital autonomy. At the moment European Commission allows data transfer to third countries outside the EU, which it recognises to offer adequate data protection and security. Some of these countries are Uruguay, US, New Zealand, Israel, Argentina, Canada, Switzerland etc.[70]

Information Technology Act, 2000

The Information Technology (IT) Act 2000,[71] was the first statutory measure taken by the GoI to regulate IT sector and protect the rights of the citizen. Section 43A of the IT Act 2000 provides a regulatory framework for the protection and maintenance of the privacy of the data of the citizens being handled by a body corporate in its computer resource. It makes any corporate body or legal person handling citizen data accountable for maintaining reasonable security practices and procedures, and preventing wrongful loss to stake holders and further, wrongful gain to any person. The Section 43A of the Act provides for damages in case of breach of data privacy. The provisions of the new Digital Personal and Data Protection Act 2023 now have replaced the provisions of Section 43A.

Further, Section 46 of the Act provides for the creation of an adjudication system headed by a GoI officer of the rank of Director, with the jurisdiction to grant damages up to INR 5 cr.

Sections 66, 66A, 66B, 66C, 66D, 66E, 66F, 67A, and 67B of the Act deal with various offences related to misuse of computers and computer resources, including publishing misleading information, stealing computer resource, causing identity theft, impersonation, violation of privacy, cyber terrorism and pornography, and sharing explicit material, including that of children.

Sections 69, 69A, 69B of the Act provides power to a central and state government officer to intercept, monitor, block public access, collect traffic data any information through computer resources in the interest of the sovereignty and integrity of the country, or the defence of the country, or to prevent incitement to contain cognisable offence and to preserve interest of friendly foreign nation etc.

The Apex Court, in Shreya Singhal V UoI,[72] which related to online publication of content, struck down the provision of Section 66A of the IT Act 2000 and has invalidated it. The judgement was passed by a two-judge bench which did not find the argument valid that Section 66A of the IT Act 2000 imposes reasonable restrictions under Article 19(2) of the Constitution of India. Justice Nariman mentioned that the provisions of the Section 66A are vague and way too broad. The court also looked down upon Section 79 of the Act and Rules 3(4) of the Intermediary guidelines, and stated that content by intermediary should only be removed under orders of the court or government authority. The same was emphasised again vide People's Union for Civil Liberties vs Union of India.[73]

Institutional Measures by Indian Government

To overcome the shortcomings and in compliance with Sections 70A and 70B of the IT Act 2000, the GoI, through the Department of Electronic and Information Technology, has promulgated National Cyber Security Policy (NCSP) in 2013[74] in order to protect the personal information of its citizens. The intention was to protect sovereign data, prevent instances of cyber fraud and fraudulent financial transaction happening in cyber-space. The measures were in addition to the IT Act, 2000.[75] The main objectives of the policy were to secure the cyber-ecosystem in the country and enable secure IT Based transactions, to create a policy-framework for designing security policies and compliance with global standards, and to create 24 x 7 response mechanism to tackle cyber threats at national and sectoral level. As a consequence of the policy, various institutions in India were created to tackle the issue of cyber threats. As per the statement made by the Hon'ble Union Minister of State for Home Affairs Shri Kiren Rijju in Lok Sabha, in reply to a question, the role of some of the institutions in defending cyber threats in India are as follows:[76]

• National Critical Information Infrastructure Protection Centre (NCIIPC). The mandate of the NCIIPC is to protect critical information infrastructure.

• The Computer Emergency Response Team (CERT-in), CERT-in has been created to coordinate efforts required in case of crisis. Its primary role is to create alerts and advisories on the latest threats from time to time. In case of a cyber threat to national assets, CERT-in will activate and coordinate efforts required with sectoral CERTs-in and act as an umbrella organisation. CERT-In has entered into a memorandum of understanding with institutions of various countries to exchange information pertaining to new threats arising, best practices and finding a solution to existing threat being faced.

• The National Cyber Security Coordinator along with the National Security Council Secretariat functions at the national level and coordinates with various agencies at the national level on issues pertaining to National Cyber-Security.

• Cyber Forensic cum Training Laboratories for cyber-crime investigation were established in states and Union territories under the Cyber Crime Prevention for Women and Children Scheme.

• A division under the Ministry of Home Affairs has been created to deal with cyber and information security.

• National Cyber Coordination Centre (NCCC). The NCCC has been created to generate necessary situational awareness for future and existing cyber threats, and to enable the sharing of information for pro-active and preventive measures by individual organisations and institutions.

• Cyber Swachhta Kendra (Botnet Cleaning and malware Analysis Centre) provides the necessary free tools to clean malware and malicious program free of cost.

The NCSP 2013, calls for a public-private partnership to adopt best practices, to develop human resources and infrastructure to tackle future cyber threats. It calls for building and evolving mechanisms to obtain strategic information regarding cyber-threats to information and communication infrastructure and creating a response mechanism, including research and development by creating centre of excellence and collaborating with industry and academia.[77]

To understand the threat originating from cyberspace and the digital domain and to protect national assets and citizen's right and data, the GoI has further created think tanks under the Ministry of Defence like the Manohar Parrikar Institute for Defence Studies and Analyses and

Cybersecurity Centre of Excellence. The centre undertakes research, issues policy briefs, web commentaries, research papers etc., on key issues related to cyberspace. It undertakes deliberations and dialogue among prominent personalities in the cyberspace through round table conferences, workshops, seminars and international conference with participation from wide stakeholders and academia.[78]

The Ministry of Defence, GoI has also created its own cyber offensive wing, a tri-service command called the Defence Cyber Agency (DCA), which is headquartered in New Delhi. The DCA is headed by a two-star rank officer reporting to the Integrated Defence Staff.[79]

Information Technology (Intermediary Guidelines and Digital Media Ethics Code) Rules, 2021

The Ministry of Electronics and Information Technology, vide Notification dated 25th Feb 2021, has promulgated the IT (Intermediary Guidelines and Digital Media Ethics Code) Rules, 2021.[80] The rules were promulgated to overcome the statutory shortcomings in India's cyber laws particularly in Information Technology Act 2000, regarding issues pertaining to data localisation and data privacy of Indian citizens by the cyber intermediaries. As per the statement made by Minister of State Shree Rajeev Chandrashekhar,[81] the policy helped the GoI to overcome statutory shortcomings in terms of cyber intermediaries' unchallenged right to suspend social media account of any citizen, spreading unconfirmed news and information that could lead to misinformation and catastrophic political consequences. The policy also addresses statutory shortcomings pertaining to complaints regarding the posting of objectionable content on social media to protect the rights of the citizens under Articles 14, 19 and 21 of the Indian Constitution.

The Rule 2 of the IT (Intermediary Guidelines and Digital Media Ethics Code) Rules, 2021 contains the definition clauses.

The Rule 2(i) defines digital media as:

Digital media means digitised content that can be transmitted over the internet or computer networks and includes content received, stored, transmitted, edited or processed by:

- An intermediary; or

- A publisher of news and current affairs content or a publisher of online curated content.

The Rule 2(v) defines 'social media intermediary as:

'significant social media intermediary means a social media intermediary having number of registered users in India above such threshold as notified by the central government.'

The Rule 2(w) of the rules define 'social media intermediary' as:

'social media intermediary means an intermediary that primarily or solely enables online interaction between two or more users and allows them to create, upload, share, disseminate, modify or access information using its service.'

The new IT Rules 2021, enumerate action for due diligence required by the intermediaries as well as social media intermediaries while discharging their duties in Rule 3, 4 and 5 of the said rules. It involves a pro-active disclosure of privacy policies on their websites. An intermediary is obligated to inform its user against publishing prohibited and harmful content with special emphasis on pornographic, obscene paedophilic content, contents that violates privacy rights, encourages crime, or threatens national sovereignty and integrity, or contain viruses or malware, and from publishing false and untrue information to injure or harass a person.

As per Rule 3(e) it is pertinent to note that temporary, transient or intermediate storage of data or information done owing to an algorithm, or done in an automated manner without the involvement of humans will not amount to hosting, storing, and publishing of any prohibited information. Further, under Rule 3(h), the intermediary is to hold the information of the registered user for 180 days.

The Rule 3(2) provides for grievance redressal mechanisms by the intermediaries including the appointment of a grievance officer and publishing his contact details and mechanism to enable users to make complaints against violations of the provisions. The section provides for acknowledgement of a complaint within 24 hours of receipt and disposal within 15 days. It also provides for action by intermediary when any notice or direction is received by a government agency.

The Section 7 provides for penal action against an intermediary if he fails to act in accordance with the laid down rules.

The IT Rules 2021 have laid down the guidelines for the curated content in their schedule. As per Rule 2(q) online curated content is defined as:

> 'Online curated content' means any curated catalogue of audio-visual content, other than news and current affairs content, that is owned by, licensed to or contracted to be transmitted by a publisher online curated content, and made available in demand,

including but not limited through subscriptions, over the internet or computer networks, and included films, audio visual programmes, documentaries, television programmes, serials, podcasts and other such content'

As per the IT Rules 2021 an online publisher may not publish or transmit any content prohibited by any law, court or competent authority. He is also supposed to exercise due caution and discretion in relation to content that affects territorial sovereignty, integrity and friendly relations with foreign countries, or content that is likely to disturb public order. All the content shall be classified based on age, suitability and nature of content especially themes involving violence, nudity, sex, language, drug and substance abuse, horror etc.

The Digital Personal Data Protection Act 2023

In order to supplement shortcoming of the IT Act 2000 pertaining to issues arising from a lack of data localisation for transnational movement of citizen data, the Digital Personal Data Protection Act 2023[82] was introduced. The intention was to protect the personal data of online users collected and processed by cyber intermediaries, and also to regulate data processing by a statute. The Ministry or Electronics and Information Technology, GoI has drafted the Act. The key features of the proposed Act include the following:

- The primary objective of the Act is to create a comprehensive framework pertaining to collecting, sharing and storing of personal digital data and its protection.

- The Act is applicable to personal data collected from users online, or offline digitised data called data principal.

•	The proposed Act puts responsibility on the data fiduciary i.e., anyone who alone or in conjunction determines the means and purpose of processing personal data.

•	The Act lays down the obligation of data fiduciary and makes him responsible to comply with provision of the Act irrespective of the agreement accepted between him and the data principle. As per the Act, the data fiduciary is obliged to maintain the accuracy and integrity of the data collected. He is supposed to maintain adequate technical safeguards. The data principle is entitled to access information collected by the data fiduciary.

•	The data fiduciary is to take consent explicitly and in plain language for every act of collection and processing of data. The withdrawal of consent shall require data fiduciary to cease processing the information collected. The Act proposes to define 'deemed consent' under various circumstances elaborately.

•	The Act puts an obligation on data fiduciary to put an institutional mechanism to ensure the personal data of individual remains protected and privacy is maintained. It further puts obligation on data fiduciary to make proactive disclosures on account of data breach to the board as well as to the data principal.

•	The Act further makes data fiduciary to delete and cease retention of data as soon as the purpose for giving of data ceases, or is no longer necessary. The data fiduciary is to publish its contact information and have a grievance redressal mechanism.

Conclusion and Recommendations

The armed forces are the primary and ultimate guardians of national security, and are often called upon to deal with unforeseen national threats; often at short notice. Digitisation has now penetrated every conceivable aspect of human life and activity. In the event of a tangible, declared war, or threat to national security due to an undeclared and/or mass cyber-attack on the nation's digital assets, the armed forces would be called upon to counter the attack and respond appropriately, post haste. In order to do so they must have the right tools, skilled manpower and requisite expertise in place. Cyber-attacks are becoming increasingly difficult to detect, identify and defend against. In today's post IT revolution 5G-6G world, where virtual reality can be teamed with AI and comingled with misinformation laced cunningly with disinformation it may become even more difficult to differentiate fact from fiction, to timely detect a threat and to defend one's assets effectively. In the present no peace no war scenario that India faces from its adversaries, the threat of pre-emptory and disabling cyber-attacks is an increasing and inescapable reality. This will eventually have to be shouldered and countered by the armed forces as the last bastion of national defence.

The digital technology's deep penetration in all interactions of human society has made it an important medium for administration and governance. The use of internet-based technologies has an extensive uses in economic, communication and trade of the nation. Therefore, these technologies need to be safe, secure and freely accessible to citizens. Any control or restriction imposed on these technologies by cyber intermediaries or a foreign adversary can have far reaching or disastrous consequences.

At the individual level, every citizen's digital asset, including his computer, private network, phone, bank account, contacts etc, being inter-connected online, are vulnerable and prone to being compromised through hacking and cyber-attacks. Any society's excessive reliance on non-indigenous digital platforms and vulnerability to the private data of any of its entities are a cause of concern for national security. The private information of a nation's innumerable entities available to cyber intermediaries, through their servers located transnationally, provides an effective, disabling tool for cyber warfare in the hands of adversaries. The digital footprints of the society can be analysed using data analytics tools by cyber intermediaries, which are usually big IT giants with tools such as bots and AI to analyse user preferences, likes and dislikes, capabilities and weaknesses, as well as to detect a wealth of scientific and technological data as part of industrial and scientific espionage. This information provides a huge data resource to the cyber intermediaries, who continue to use this data for their own economic and business gain or share them with third party with scant regard to other's national security and individual's privacy. This information is sourced by foreign intelligence agencies and deep state to cause political turmoil and to gain immediate tactical and strategic advantage during wars.

Cyber intermediaries having their servers located in different countries across the world, cause transnational migration of data of large number of citizens and cities, thereby, exposing the vulnerabilities of a state to foreign adversaries. These vulnerabilities, in the present age, are amplified by advanced analytical and imaging tools, and with the use of advanced technologies, including AI.

Many nations across the globe have strict regulatory control over the migration of citizen data across the borders, especially in nations such as Russia, China and many developed countries. GoI is rightly concerned about making cyber intermediaries accountable to ensure the privacy and security of its citizen's data by enacting various laws. Even the Supreme Court of India, through its various judgements, has placed high importance on an individual's right to privacy. The Apex Court, in Justice K.S. Puttaswamy V. Union of India, has held that an invasion of privacy must be fair, for legitimate reason and reasonable. The Apex Court has further held that the right to privacy is an extension of fundamental rights enshrined in Article 21 of the Indian Constitution. In Kaushal Kishore V. State of UP,[83] the Apex Court has held that held that the fundamental rights can be enforced against private individuals. The cyber intermediaries are thus accountable to Indian citizens when handling their data. The GoI has instituted various measures to ensure the safety of citizens' data, as the same has a direct bearing on national security. India at present does not have adequate statutory safeguards to compel data localisation that prevents its movement across the border. The merit of any such statutory provision, if brought in by legislation, has to be studied in conjunction with economic viability vis-à-vis national security. Some new measures have been taken through the enactment of new statutes and rules like the NCSP 2013, and the Digital Personal Data Protection Act 2023, which makes intermediaries, social intermediaries and data fiduciary accountable for the way they handle citizens' data. The Government of India has also established various institutions like the Defence Cyber Command, NCCC,

NCSC, and CERT-In etc., for the protection of citizens' data, IT infrastructure, to respond in case of cyber-attacks and to seek enforcement of various IT laws.

The premiere Indian institutions, like the All India Institute of Medical Sciences and the Kundakulam nuclear plant, continue to face cyber-attacks without adequate defence mechanisms. Additionally, the high reliance on foreign software applications, OS, social media application and digital resources provided by foreign intermediaries are a great cause of concern as they remain our sources of vulnerabilities. The solution lies in leveraging the Indian IT industry, developing and promoting Indian applications, OS and software systems and building robust domestic IT software and hardware to cater to domestic needs. This would require great foresight, considerable government initiative and citizens' awareness and support. The government would have to collaborate with IT giants and corporate big-wigs in India to come out with local solutions, adequate regulatory and defensive measures.

The armed forces and security agencies will have to develop their own capabilities, skills, tools and trained manpower, in parallel, to counter new emerging threats in the cyber domain. Offence is the best defence. The evolution of AI with quantum computing technology poses its own risks and offers opportunity. India has to develop its own safety institutes to collaborate with advanced western nation. The government agencies would necessarily have to collaborate and if necessary even finance such research, with corporates and IT giants to counter AI based threats whilst developing their own AI based resources and tools for information warfare. The Chinese have made tremendous strides in advanced technologies, including the widespread use and application of 5G, AI and automation among others. India must learn from both, its adversaries and other leaders in the field, to realise the potential of emerging technologies and stay ahead in the race. Rapid development, use and promotion of indigenous AI and quantum systems is the need of the hour and must be on high priority of the government agencies including the armed forces. The same has wide applications across industry, military, space, medicine, surveillance, research and development. Therefore, new emerging technologies must be absorbed and exploited to their highest potential to keep the nation ahead in the race. Needless to say, our cyber laws must also evolve with time, not only to protect and safeguard our cyber sphere from outside interference, but also to play a leading role in defining international norms as a world leader in cyber science and technologies.

Endnotes

1   Frank Hofmann, "*Israel shows Hamas terror videos to document horrific attack*", DW, available at *https://www.dw.com/en/israel-shows-hamas-terror-videos-to-document-horrific-attack/a-67305110 (Last visited on 06 Dec 2023)*

2   Emanuel Fabian, "*Hamas's main operations base is under Shifa Hospital in Gaza City*", The Times of Israel, available at https://www.timesofisrael.com/hamass-main-operations-base-is-under-shifa-hospital-in-gaza-city-says-idf/ (Last visited on 06 Nov 2023)

3   "Defence Cyber Command", SP's aviation, available at https://www.sps-aviation.com/experts-speak/?id=554, (last visited on 06 Nov 2023)

4   Nik Martin, *How US, China COVID recovery dwarfs all others*, DW https://www.dw.com/en/us-china-covid-recovery-dwarfs-all-others/a-60334211 (Last visited 29 Jan 2023)

5   Brenden Hoffman, *Global economic Uncertainty Remains Elevated, Weighing on Growth*, IMF BLOG https://www.imf.org/en/Blogs/Articles/2023/01/26/global-economic-uncertainty-remains-elevated-weighing-on-growth (Last visited 29 Jan 2023)

6   *UK Economy Latest*, OFFICE OF NATIONAL STATISTICS, https://www.ons.gov.uk/economy/economicoutputandproductivity/output/articles/ukeconomylatest/2021-01-25 (Last visited 29 Jan 2023)

7   Reuters, *German economic institutes cut 2023 GDP forecast on energy price surge*, REUTERS https://www.reuters.com/world/europe/germanys-ifw-predicts-recession-record-inflation-2023-2022-09-08/ (Last visited 29 Jan 2023)

8   Nikita Rana, *India an oasis for investors: ETILC and HSBC Roundtable*, THE ECONOMIC TIMES, https://economictimes.indiatimes.com/news/company/corporate-trends/india-an-oasis-for-investors-etilc-and-hsbc-roundtable/articleshow/94326408.cms?from=mdr   (Last visited on 29 Jan 2023)

9   India to be USD 5 trillion economy by FY 2026: CEA Anantha Nageswaran, The Economic Times, *GDP Growth(annual%)-India*, https://economictimes.indiatimes.com/news/economy/finance/

india-to-be-usd-5-trillion-economy-by-fy2026-cea-anantha-nageswaran/articleshow/97500680.cms (last visited on 12 dec 2023)

10 PTI, *Digitisation a game changer for Indian economy, says IMF Chief economist,* THE ECONOMIC TIMES https://economictimes.indiatimes.com/news/india/digitisation-a-game-changer-for-indian-economy-says-imf-chief-economist/articleshow/94821624.cms (Last visited on 30 Jan 2023)

11 *The Global Information Technology Report 2013,* WORLD ECONOMIC FORUM, https://www3.weforum.org/docs/GITR/2013/GITR_Chapter1.2_2013.pdf (Last visited 28 Jan 2023)

12 *ASEAN Digital Generation Report: Digital Financial inclusion,* WORLD ECONOMIC FORUM, December 2022

13 *Using Digital Technology for a Green and Just recovery in Cities-Insight Report,* WORLD ECONOMIC FORUM, August 2022, p7, para 1.1.

14 Digital Payments and Their Impact on the Indian Economy, IBEF, https://www.ibef.org/research/case-study/digital-payments-and-their-impact-on-the-indian-economy (Last visited on 29 Jan 2023)

15 Ministry of Electronics and Information Technology, Government of India, https://meity.dashboard.nic.in (Last visited on 28 Jan 2023)

16 Supra 15

17 ibid

18 *Using Digital Technology for a Green and Just recovery in Cities-Insight Report,* WORLD ECONOMIC FORUM, August 2022, p16, para 3.1.

19 Global Cybersecurity Outlook 2022 insight report, WORLD ECONOMIC FORUM, January 2022, P13, para 1.1.

20 Kate Fazzini, Tom Dichristopher, *An alarmingly simple cyberattack hit electriacl system serving LA and Salt Lake, But Power Never went down,* CNBC https://www.cnbc.com/2019/05/02/ddos-attack-caused-interruptions-in-power-system-operations-doe.html (Last visited on 03 Feb 2023)

21 Robert Walton, Sophisticated hackers could crash the US power grid, but money, not sabotage, is their focus, UTILITY DIVE https://www.utilitydive.com/news/sophisticated-hackers-could-crash-the-

us-power-grid-but-money-not-sabotag/603764/ (last visited on 03 Feb 2023)

22   Aishwarya Paliwal, *Had informed govt about Kundakulam nuclear power plant cyber attack: Former NTRO Cyber security analyst*, INDIA TODAY https://www.indiatoday.in/india/story/had-informed-govt-about-kudankulam-nuclear-power-plant-cyber-attack-former-ntro-cyber-security-analyst-1616304-2019-11-06 (Last visited on 03 Feb 2023)

23   Akshaye Dongare, Delhi AIIMS server hacked by Chines, data safe now: Govt source, India Today https://www.indiatoday.in/india/story/server-attack-delhi-aiims-chinese-fir-2309052-2022-12-14 (Last Visited on 03 Feb 2023)

24   Lena Firestone, *Understanding Cell Phone Addiction,* PSYCHALIVE https://www.psychalive.org/cell-phone-addiction/ (last visited on 03 Feb 2023)

25   *Using Digital Technology for a Green and Just recovery in Cities-Insight Report*, WORLD ECONOMIC FORUM, August 2022, p16, Fig 2

26   Adrian Shahbaz and Allie Funk, *Freedom on the NET 2019-The Crisis of Social Media*, FREEDOM HOUSE *https://www.freedomonthenet. org/sites/default/files/2019-11/11042019_Report_FH_FOTN_2019_ final_Public_Download.pdf (Last visited on 31 Jan 2023)*

27   Dan Goodin, *Android 20X more data to Google than iOS send to Apple, study says,* ARS TECHNICA https://arstechnica.com/gadgets/2021/03/android-sends-20x-more-data-to-google-than-ios-sends-to-apple-study-says/ (Last visited on 03 Feb 2023)

28   Douglas J Leith, *Mobile Handset Privacy: Measuring The Data iOS and Android Send to Apple And Google*, School of Computer Science and Statistics, Trinity College Dublin, Ireland, 25 Mar 2021 https://www.scss.tcd.ie/doug.leith/apple_google.pdf   (last visited 03 Feb 2023)

29   Naveen Goud, *Elon Musk destroys his phone regularly due to Data Security Fears*, CYBERSECURITY INSIDERS, (28 Jan 2023,11:36 hrs IST),   https://www.cybersecurity-insiders.com/elon-musk-destroys-his-phone-regularly-due-to-data-security-fears/

30 Katie Holmes, *How to track individual users in Google Analytics*, Ruler Analytics https://www.ruleranalytics.com/blog/analytics/google-analytics-user-tracking/ (last visited 01 Feb 2023)

31 *Welcome to Google Analytics for beginner,* Google Analytics https://www.youtube.com/watch?v=GG5xBwbje1E*(Last visited on 01 Feb 2023)*

32 Ajay Agarwal, Joshua Gans, Avi Goldfarb, "Chat GPT and How AI Disrupts Industries", Harward Business Review, available at https://hbr.org/2022/12/chatgpt-and-how-ai-disrupts-industries, Last visited on 16 Oct 2023.

33 Ed Newton-Rex, Medium, *59 impressive things artificial intelligence can do today,* available at https://www.businessinsider.com/artificial-intelligence-ai-most-impressive-achievements-2017-3?IR=T, (Last visited on 01 Jul 2023)

34 Sing Yong Teng, Guo Yong Yew, *"Microalgae with artificial intelligence: A Digitalized perspective on genetics, systems and products"*, Biotechnology Advances, Elsevier Vol 44, 15 Nov 2020, available at https://www.sciencedirect.com/science/article/abs/pii/S0734975020301336 (Last visited on 17 Oct 2023)

35 Roxana Motorga, Vlad Muresan, "Artificial Intelligence in Fractional-Order Systems Approximation with High Performances: Application in Modelling of an ISOTOPIC Separation Process", MDPI, available at https://www.mdpi.com/2227-7390/10/9/1459, (Last visited on 17 Oct 2023)

36 Matt Egan, *Exclusive: 42% of CEO says AI could destroy humanity in five to ten years.* CNN Business, available at https://edition.cnn.com/2023/06/14/business/artificial-intelligence-ceos-warning/index.html (last visited on 01 Jul 2023)

37 *What are the most pressing dangers of AI?,* Standford Universit, available at https://ai100.stanford.edu/2021-report/standing-questions-and-responses/sq10-what-are-most-pressing-dangers-ai (Last visited on 01 Jul 2023)

38 Christy DeSmith, *why China has edge on AI, what ancient emperor tell us about Xi Jingping,* The Harvard Gazette, https://news.harvard.edu/gazette/story/2023/03/why-china-has-an-edge-on-artificial-intelligence/ (Last visited on 01 Jul 2023)

39 Kai Shen, Xiaoxiao, *The next frontier for AI in China could add $600 billion to its economy*, Quantum Back AI by McKinsey available at https://www.mckinsey.com/capabilities/quantumblack/our-insights/the-next-frontier-for-ai-in-china-could-add-600-billion-to-its-economy (Last visited on 01 Jul 2023)

40 *"The Sunak, Musk and AI: What we learned from the Bletchley Park Summit"*, The Gaurdian, available at https://www.theguardian.com/technology/2023/nov/03/rishi-sunak-elon-musk-ai-summit-what-we-learned (Last visited on 06 Nov 2023)

41 Bijin Jose, *"Rishi Sunak asks Elon Musk tough questions on AI: 6 Key things discussed"*. The Indian Express, available at https://indianexpress.com/article/technology/artificial-intelligence/rishi-sunak-elon-musk-uk-ai-safety-summit-9013125/, (Last visited on 06 Nov 2023).

42 Amit Chaturvedi, "Rishi Sunak says AI could make it easier to build chemical weapons", NDTVWORLD available at https://www.ndtv.com/world-news/rishi-sunak-says-ai-could-make-it-easier-to-build-chemical-weapons-4516511 (last visited on 06 Nov 2023)

43 Reuters, *"United States to launch its own AI safety institute"*, Hindustan Times, available at https://www.hindustantimes.com/world-news/united-states-to-launch-its-own-ai-safety-institute-101698873560237.html, (Last visited on 06 Nov 2023)

44 *"what is quantum computing"*, IBM , available at https://www.ibm.com/topics/quantum-computing (last visited on 01 Jul 2023)

45 Thomas Corbett, Peter W Singer, *China may have just taken the lead in the quantum computing race*, Defense One, https://www.defenseone.com/ideas/2022/04/china-may-have-just-taken-lead-quantum-computing-race/365707/ (last visited on 01 Jul 2023)

46 *How social media is using artificial Intelligence in 2020*, CURVEARRO https://www.curvearro.com/blog/how-social-media-is-using-artificial-intelligence-in-2020/ (last Visited on 08 Feb 2023)

47 Jeff Loucks, "Deepfakes and AI-Questioning artificial intelligence ethics and the dangers of AI", Deloitte, available at https://www2.deloitte.com/us/en/pages/technology-media-and-telecommunications/articles/deepfakes-artificial-intelligence-ethics.html (Last visited on 17 Oct 2023).

48 *Press Release No. 55/2022-23 dated 2.10.2022*, Competition Commission of India, https://www.cci.gov.in/antitrust/press-release/details/261/0 (Last visited on 03 Feb 2022)

49 Rhoda Wilson, *Twitter aided US Intelligence agencies to influence foreign governments.* THE EXPOSE, https://expose-news.com/2023/01/03/twitter-aided-us-intel-to-influence-foreign-governments/ (Last Visited on 03 Feb 2023)

50 Global Cybersecurity Outlook 2022 insight report, WORLD ECONOMIC FORUM, January 2022, P12, Fig 3

51 Foo Yun Chee, John Chalmers, *Google, Facebook, Twitter must combat fake news-Polish, Baltic Leaders,* REUTERS https://www.reuters.com/technology/google-facebook-twitter-must-combat-ukraine-fake-news-polish-baltic-leaders-2022-02-28/ (Last Visited 03 Feb 2023)

52 Jeff Schogol, *Russian soldier gave away his position with geotagged social media posts,* TASK and PURPOSE https://taskandpurpose.com/news/russian-military-opsec-failure-ukraine/ (Last Visited on 03 Feb 2023)

53 Web Desk, *Did Modi Government deduce Balakot Fatalities from number of active mobile phones,* THE WEEK https://www.theweek.in/news/india/2019/03/06/modi-govt-deduce-balakot-fatalities-active-mobile-phones.html (last visited 03 Feb 2023)

54 Natalie Huet, *Which tech companies are cutting ties with Russia over its war in Ukraine?*, EURONEWS.NEXT https://www.euronews.com/next/2022/03/17/which-tech-companies-are-cutting-ties-with-russia-over-its-war-in-ukraine

55 Brig Pawan Bhardwaj, YSM , *"Strategic Buyouts Supports Strategic Communication".* Strategic Perspective, USI, available at https://www.usiofindia.org/strategic-perspective/Strategic-Buyouts-Support-Strategic-Communication.html (Last visited on 17 Oct 2023)

56 ibid

57 Theo Wayt, *Google Disables maps tools in Ukraine used to track troops, civilians,* NEW YORK POST https://nypost.com/2022/02/28/google-disables-maps-tools-in-ukraine-to-track-troops-civilians/ (Last visited 05 Feb 2023

58   Ishan Srivastav, *How Kargil spurred India to design own GPS*, TIMES OF INDIA https://timesofindia.indiatimes.com/home/science/How-Kargil-spurred-India-to-design-own-GPS/articleshow/33254691.cms (Last visited 05 February 2023)

59   India Const. art 21

60   Kaushal Kishore V. State of UP 2023Livelaw(SC)4 WP(Crl) No. 113/2016

61   Kharak Singh V. State of U.P AIR1963 SC 1295

62   Govind Singh V. State of M.P 1975AIR1378, 1975SCR(3)946

63   People's Union for Civil Liberties v. Union of India AIR 1997SC568

64   Unique Identification Authority of India andAnr. V. Central Bureau of Investigation Special Leave to Appeal(Crl)No(s.)2524/2014 order dated 24 mar 2014

65   Justice K.S. Puttaswamy V Union of India (2017)10 SCC 1

66   Nigel Cory, *Cross-Border Data Flows: Where are the Barriers, and what do they cost?*, ITIF https://itif.org/publications/2017/05/01/cross-border-data-flows-where-are-barriers-and-what-do-they-cost/ (Last visited on 01 Feb 2023)

67   Adrian Shahbaz and Allie Funk, *Freedom on the NET 2019-The Crisis of Social Media*, FREEDOM HOUSE p5 *https://www.freedomonthenet.org/sites/default/files/2019-11/11042019_Report_FH_FOTN_2019_final_Public_Download.pdf (Last visited on 31 Jan 2023)*

68   Adam Smith, *Russia will force Facebook and Twitter to keep data on its citizens within the country.* INDEPENDENT https://www.independent.co.uk/tech/russia-facebook-twitter-data-b1854189.html (last visited on 01 Feb 2023)

69   Nigel Cory, *Cross-Border Data Flows: Where are the Barriers, and what do they cost?*, ITIF https://itif.org/publications/2017/05/01/cross-border-data-flows-where-are-barriers-and-what-do-they-cost/ (Last visited on 05 Feb 2023)

70   Nigel Cory, *Cross-Border Data Flows: Where are the Barriers, and what do they cost?*, ITIF https://itif.org/publications/2017/05/01/

cross-border-data-flows-where-are-barriers-and-what-do-they-cost/ (Last visited on 05 Feb 2023)

71   Information Technology Act, 2000, No.21, Acts of Parliament, 2000(India)

72   Shreya Singhal V UoI (2015)5 SCC 1

73   People's Union for Civil Liberties v Union of India MA 901/2021in W.P.(Crl) No.199/2013, 2022 Livelaw (SC) 846

74   *Notification on National Cyber Security Policy-2013, File No. 2(35)/2011-CERT-In dated 02 Jul 2013*, DEPARTMENT OF ELECTRONICS AND INFORMATION TECHNOLOGY, MINISTRY OF COMMUNICATION AND INFORMATION Technology   https://www.meity.gov.in/sites/upload_files/dit/files/National%20Cyber%20Security%20Policy%20%281%29.pdf   (Last visited on 05 Feb 2023)

75   The information Technology Act, 2000, No 21, Acts of Parliament, 2000(India)

76   Union Minister of State for Home Affairs, Shri Kiren Rijju, *Cyber Security-Ministry of Home Affairs,* PRESS INFORMATION BUREAU https://pib.gov.in/PressReleaseIframePage.aspx?PRID=1556474 ?(Last Visited 06 Feb 2023)

77   Lt Col Sanjiv Tomar, *national Cyber Security Policy 2013: An Assessment,* Manohar Parrikar Institute for Defence Studies and Analysis, https://www.idsa.in/idsacomments/NationalCyberSecurityPolicy2013_stomar_260813 (Last visited on 05 Feb 2023)

78   *Manohar Parrikar IDSA Cybersecurity Centre of Excellence(ICCOE),* Manohar Parrikar Institute For defence Studies and Analysis. https://www.idsa.in/idsa_ICCOE (Last visited on 05 Feb 2023)

79   Lt Gen(retd) DS Hooda, *India's New Defence Cyber Agency will have to work around stovepipes built by Army, Navy and Air Force.* NEWS18   https://www.news18.com/news/opinion/new-defence-cyber-agency-will-have-to-work-around-stovepipes-built-by-army-navy-air-force-lt-gen-hooda-2204033.html (Last visited on 6 Feb 2023

80   Extraordinary Gazette of India CG-DL-E-25022021-225464 dated 25 Feb 2021, Ministry of Information and Broadcasting https://mib.gov.in/sites/default/files/Digital%20Media%20Ethics%20Code%20

Rules%20%20Notification%20%281%29.pdf (Last visited on 06 Feb 2023)

81   Statement by Minister of State Shree Rajeev Chandrashekhar dated 29 Oct 2022, Press Information Bureau, Government of India https://pib.gov.in/PressReleaseIframePage.aspx?PRID=1871840

82   The Digital Personal Data Protection Act, 2023(Act 22 of 2023)

83   Kaushal Kishore V. State of UP 2023Livelaw(SC)4 WP(Crl) No. 113/2016

References and Bibliography

1.   **ARTICLES/ REPORTS/ NEWS REPORTS/ RESEARCH PAPERS**

(a)   Frank Hofmann, *"Israel shows Hamas terror videos to document horrific attack"*, DW, available at https://www.dw.com/en/israel-shows-hamas-terror-videos-to-document-horrific-attack/a-67305110 (Last visited on 06 Dec 2023)

(b)   Emanuel Fabian, *"Hamas's main operations base is under Shifa Hospital in Gaza City"*, The Times of Israel, available at https://www.timesofisrael.com/hamass-main-operations-base-is-under-shifa-hospital-in-gaza-city-says-idf/ (Last visited on 06 Nov 2023)

(c)   "Defence Cyber Command", SP's aviation, available at https://www.sps-aviation.com/experts-speak/?id=554, (last visited on 06 Nov 2023)

(d)   Nik Martin, *"How US, China COVID recovery dwarfs all others"*, DW, available at https://www.dw.com/en/us-china-covid-recovery-dwarfs-all-others/a-60334211 (Last visited 29 Jan 2023)

(e)   Brenden Hoffman, *"Global economic Uncertainty Remains Elevated, Weighing on Growth"*, IMF BLOG https://www.imf.org/en/Blogs/Articles/2023/01/26/global-economic-uncertainty-remains-elevated-weighing-on-growth (Last visited 29 Jan 2023)

(f)   *UK Economy Latest,* OFFICE OF NATIONAL STATISTICS,   https://www.ons.gov.uk/economy/

economicoutputandproductivity/output/articles/ ukeconomylatest/2021-01-25 (Last visited 29 Jan 2023)

(g) Reuters, *"German economic institutes cut 2023 GDP forecast on energy price surge"*, REUTERS https://www.reuters.com/ world/europe/germanys-ifw-predicts-recession-record-inflation-2023-2022-09-08/ (Last visited 29 Jan 2023)

(h) Nikita Rana, *"India an oasis for investors: ETILC and HSBC Roundtable"*, THE ECONOMIC TIMES, https:// economictimes.indiatimes.com/news/company/corporate-trends/india-an-oasis-for-investors-etilc-and-hsbc-roundtable/ articleshow/94326408.cms?from=mdr (Last visited on 29 Jan 2023)

(i) *The Global Information Technology Report 2013*, WORLD ECONOMIC FORUM, https://www3.weforum.org/docs/ GITR/2013/GITR_Chapter1.2_2013.pdf (Last visited 28 Jan 2023)

(j) *ASEAN Digital Generation Report: Digital Financial inclusion*, WORLD ECONOMIC FORUM, December 2022

(k) *Using Digital Technology for a Green and Just recovery in Cities-Insight Report*, WORLD ECONOMIC FORUM, August 2022.

(l) *Digital Payments and Their Impact on the Indian Economy*, IBEF, https://www.ibef.org/research/case-study/digital-payments-and-their-impact-on-the-indian-economy (Last visited on 29 Jan 2023)

(m) *Using Digital Technology for a Green and Just recovery in Cities-Insight Report*, WORLD ECONOMIC FORUM, August 2022

(n) Global Cybersecurity Outlook 2022 insight report, WORLD ECONOMIC FORUM, January 2022

(o) Kate Fazzini, Tom Dichristopher, *An alarmingly simple cyberattack hit electrical system serving LA and Salt Lake, But Power Never went down*, CNBC, available at https://www.cnbc. com/2019/05/02/ddos-attack-caused-interruptions-in-power-system-operations-doe.html (Last visited on 03 Feb 2023)

(p) Robert Walton, *"Sophisticated hackers could crash the US power grid, but money, not sabotage, is their focus"*, UTILITY DIVE, available at https://www.utilitydive.com/news/sophisticated-hackers-could-crash-the-us-power-grid-but-money-not-sabotag/603764/ (last visited on 03 Feb 2023)

(q) Aishwarya Paliwal, *Had informed govt about Kundakulam nuclear power plant cyber attack: Former NTRO Cyber security analyst*, INDIA TODAY, available at https://www.indiatoday.in/india/story/had-informed-govt-about-kudankulam-nuclear-power-plant-cyber-attack-former-ntro-cyber-security-analyst-1616304-2019-11-06 (Last visited on 03 Feb 2023)

(r) Akshaye Dongare, *Delhi AIIMS server hacked by Chines, data safe now: Govt source*, India Today, available at https://www.indiatoday.in/india/story/server-attack-delhi-aiims-chinese-fir-2309052-2022-12-14 (Last Visited on 03 Feb 2023)

(s) *Using Digital Technology for a Green and Just recovery in Cities-Insight Report*, WORLD ECONOMIC FORUM, August 2022

(t) Adrian Shahbaz and Allie Funk, *Freedom on the NET 2019-The Crisis of Social Media*, FREEDOM HOUSE, available at https://www.freedomonthenet.org/sites/default/files/2019-11/11042019_Report_FH_FOTN_2019_final_Public_Download.pdf (Last visited on 31 Jan 2023).

(u) Dan Goodin, *Android 20X more data to Google than iOS send to Apple, study says*, ARS TECHNICA, available at https://arstechnica.com/gadgets/2021/03/android-sends-20x-more-data-to-google-than-ios-sends-to-apple-study-says/ (Last visited on 03 Feb 2023)

(v) Douglas J Leith, *Mobile Handset Privacy: Measuring The Data iOS and Android Send to Apple And Google*, School of Computer Science and Statistics, Trinity College Dublin, Ireland, 25 Mar 2021, available at https://www.scss.tcd.ie/doug.leith/apple_google.pdf (last visited 03 Feb 2023)

(w) Naveen Goud, *Elon Musk destroys his phone regularly due to Data Security Fears*, CYBERSECURITY INSIDERS, (28 Jan 2023,11:36 hrs IST), https://www.cybersecurity-insiders.com/elon-musk-destroys-his-phone-regularly-due-to-data-security-fears/

(x) Katie Holmes, *How to track individual users in Google Analytics, Ruler Analytics* https://www.ruleranalytics.com/blog/analytics/google-analytics-user-tracking/ (last visited 01 Feb 2023)

(y)   *Welcome to Google Analytics for beginner,* Google Analytics https://www.youtube.com/watch?v=GG5xBwbje1E(Last visited on 01 Feb 2023)

(z)   Ajay Agarwal, Joshua Gans, Avi Goldfarb, *"Chat GPT and How AI Disrupts Industries"*, Harward Business Review, available at https://hbr.org/2022/12/chatgpt-and-how-ai-disrupts-industries, (Last visited on 16 Oct 2023).

(aa) Ed Newton-Rex, Medium, *59 impressive things artificial intelligence can do today,* available at https://www.businessinsider.com/artificial-intelligence-ai-most-impressive-achievements-2017-3?IR=T, (Last visited on 01 Jul 2023)

(ab) Sing Yong Teng, Guo Yong Yew, *"Microalgae with artificial intelligence: A Digitalized perspective on genetics, systems and products"*, Biotechnology Advances, Elsevier Vol 44, 15 Nov 2020, available at https://www.sciencedirect.com/science/article/abs/pii/S0734975020301336 (Last visited on 17 Oct 2023)

(ac) Roxana Motorga, Vlad Muresan, *" Artificial Intelligence in Fractional-Order Systems Approximation with High Performances: Application in Modelling of an ISOTOPIC Separation Process"*, MDPI, available at https://www.mdpi.com/2227-7390/10/9/1459, (Last visited on 17 Oct 2023)

(ad) Matt Egan, Exclusive: *42% of CEO says AI could destroy humanity in five to ten years.* CNN Business, available at https://edition.cnn.com/2023/06/14/business/artificial-intelligence-ceos-warning/index.html (last visited on 01 Jul 2023)

(ae) *What are the most pressing dangers of AI?*, Standford University, available at https://ai100.stanford.edu/2021-report/standing-questions-and-responses/sq10-what-are-most-pressing-dangers-ai (Last visited on 01 Jul 2023)

(af) Christy DeSmith, *why China has edge on AI, what ancient emperor tell us about Xi Jingping,* The Harvard Gazette, https://news.harvard.edu/gazette/story/2023/03/why-china-has-an-edge-on-artificial-intelligence/ (Last visited on 01 Jul 2023)

(ag) Kai Shen, Xiaoxiao, *The next frontier for AI in China could add $600 billion to its economy,* Quantum Back AI by McKinsey available at https://www.mckinsey.com/capabilities/

quantumblack/our-insights/the-next-frontier-for-ai-in-china-could-add-600-billion-to-its-economy (Last visited on 01 Jul 2023)

(ah) *"The Sunak, Musk and AI: What we learned from the Bletchley Park Summit"*, The Gaurdian, available at https://www.theguardian.com/technology/2023/nov/03/rishi-sunak-elon-musk-ai-summit-what-we-learned (Last visited on 06 Nov 2023)

(ai) Bijin Jose, *"Rishi Sunak asks Elon Musk tough questions on AI: 6 Key things discussed"*. The Indian Express, available at https://indianexpress.com/article/technology/artificial-intelligence/rishi-sunak-elon-musk-uk-ai-safety-summit-9013125/, (Last visited on 06 Nov 2023).

(aj) Amit Chaturvedi, *"Rishi Sunak says AI could make it easier to build chemical weapons"*, NDTVWORLD available at https://www.ndtv.com/world-news/rishi-sunak-says-ai-could-make-it-easier-to-build-chemical-weapons-4516511 (last visited on 06 Nov 2023)

(ak) Reuters, *"United States to launch its own AI safety institute"*, Hindustan Times, available at https://www.hindustantimes.com/world-news/united-states-to-launch-its-own-ai-safety-institute-101698873560237.html, (Last visited on 06 Nov 2023)

(al) *"what is quantum computing"*, IBM, available at https://www.ibm.com/topics/quantum-computing (last visited on 01 Jul 2023)

(am)   Thomas Corbett, Peter W Singer, *China may have just taken the lead in the quantum computing race*, Defense One, https://www.defenseone.com/ideas/2022/04/china-may-have-just-taken-lead-quantum-computing-race/365707/ (last visited on 01 Jul 2023)

(an) *How social media is using artificial Intelligence in 2020*, CURVEARRO https://www.curvearro.com/blog/how-social-media-is-using-artificial-intelligence-in-2020/ (last Visited on 08 Feb 2023)

(ao) Jeff Loucks, *"Deepfakes and AI-Questioning artificial intelligence ethics and the dangers of AI"*, Deloitte, available at https://www2.deloitte.com/us/en/pages/technology-media-and-telecommunications/articles/deepfakes-artificial-intelligence-ethics.html (Last visited on 17 Oct 2023).

(ap) Rhoda Wilson, Twitter aided US Intelligence agencies to influence foreign governments. THE EXPOSE, https://expose-news.com/2023/01/03/twitter-aided-us-intel-to-influence-foreign-governments/ (Last Visited on 03 Feb 2023)

(aq) Global Cybersecurity Outlook 2022 insight report, WORLD ECONOMIC FORUM, January 2022.

(ar) Rhoda Wilson, *Twitter aided US Intelligence agencies to influence foreign governments.* THE EXPOSE, https://expose-news.com/2023/01/03/twitter-aided-us-intel-to-influence-foreign-governments/ (Last Visited on 03 Feb 2023)

(as) Foo Yun Chee, John Chalmers, *Google, Facebook, Twitter must combat fake news-Polish, Baltic Leaders*, REUTERS https://www.reuters.com/technology/google-facebook-twitter-must-combat-ukraine-fake-news-polish-baltic-leaders-2022-02-28/ (Last Visited 03 Feb 2023)

(at) Jeff Schogol, *Russian soldier gave away his position with geotagged social media posts*, TASK and PURPOSE https://taskandpurpose.com/news/russian-military-opsec-failure-ukraine/ (Last Visited on 03 Feb 2023)

(au) Web Desk, Did Modi Government deduce Balakot Fatalities from number of active mobile phones, THE WEEK https://www.theweek.in/news/india/2019/03/06/modi-govt-deduce-balakot-fatalities-active-mobile-phones.html (last visited 03 Feb 2023)

(av) Natalie Huet, *Which tech companies are cutting ties with Russia over its war in Ukraine?*, EURONEWS.NEXT https://www.euronews.com/next/2022/03/17/which-tech-companies-are-cutting-ties-with-russia-over-its-war-in-ukraine

(aw) Brig Pawan Bhardwaj, YSM , *"Strategic Buyouts Supports Strategic Communication"*. Strategic Perspective, USI , available at https://www.usiofindia.org/strategic-perspective/Strategic-Buyouts-Support-Strategic-Communication.html (Last visited on 17 Oct 2023) (ax) Theo Wayt, *Google Disables maps tools in Ukraine used to track troops, civilians*, NEW YORK POST https://nypost.com/2022/02/28/google-disables-maps-tools-in-ukraine-to-track-troops-civilians/ (Last visited 05 Feb 2023)

(ay) Nigel Cory, *Cross-Border Data Flows: Where are the Barriers, and what do they cost?*, ITIF available at https://itif.org/publications/2017/05/01/cross-border-data-flows-where-are-barriers-and-what-do-they-cost/ (Last visited on 01 Feb 2023)

(az) Adrian Shahbaz and Allie Funk, *Freedom on the NET 2019-The Crisis of Social Media*, FREEDOM HOUSE available at https://www.freedomonthenet.org/sites/default/files/2019-11/11042019_Report_FH_FOTN_2019_final_Public_Download.pdf (Last visited on 31 Jan 2023)

(ba) Adam Smith, *Russia will force Facebook and Twitter to keep data on its citizens within the country.* INDEPENDENT https://www.independent.co.uk/tech/russia-facebook-twitter-data-b1854189.html (last visited on 01 Feb 2023)

(bb) Lt Col Sanjiv Tomar, *National Cyber Security Policy 2013: An Assessment, Manohar Parrikar Institute for Defence Studies and Analysis*, https://www.idsa.in/idsacomments/NationalCyberSecurityPolicy2013_stomar_260813 (Last visited on 05 Feb 2023)

(bc) Lt Gen(retd) DS Hooda, *India's New Defence Cyber Agency will have to work around stovepipes built by Army, Navy and Air Force.* NEWS18 https://www.news18.com/news/opinion/new-defence-cyber-agency-will-have-to-work-around-stovepipes-built-by-army-navy-air-force-lt-gen-hooda-2204033.html (Last visited on 6 Feb 2023)

2. **WEBSITES**

(a) https://www.idsa.in/idsa_ICCOE

(b) https://www.freedomonthenet.org

(c) https://www2.deloitte.com

(d) https://nypost.com

(e) https://www.usiofindia.org

(f)   https://www.freedomonthenet.org

(g)   https://itif.org

(h)   https://www.news18.com

(i)   https://www.usiofindia.org

(j)   Ministry of Electronics and Information Technology, Government of India, https://meity.dashboard.nic.in (Last visited on 28 Jan 2023)

(k)   Manohar Parrikar IDSA Cybersecurity Centre of Excellence(ICCOE), Manohar Parrikar Institute For defence Studies and Analysis. https://www.idsa.in/idsa_ICCOE (Last visited on 05 Feb 2023)

(l)   Statement by Minister of State Shree Rajeev Chandrashekhar dated 29 Oct 2022, Press Information Bureau, Government of India https://pib.gov.in/PressReleaseIframePage.aspx?PRID=1871840

(m)   https://www.sps-aviation.com/

(n)   https://www.imf.org

3.   STATUTES/ ACTS/ GUIDELINES/ ORDERS/GAZETTE

(a)   Press Release No. 55/2022-23 dated 2.10.2022, Competition Commission of India, https://www.cci.gov.in/antitrust/press-release/details/261/0 (Last visited on 03 Feb 2022)

(b)   Information Technology Act, 2000, No.21, Acts of Parliament, 2000(India)

(c)   Notification on National Cyber Security Policy-2013, File No. 2(35)/2011-CERT-In dated 02 Jul 2013, Department Of Electronics And Information Technology, Ministry Of Communication And Information Technology, available at https://www.meity.gov.in/sites/upload_files/dit/files/National%20Cyber%20Security%20Policy%20%281%29.pdf (Last visited on 05 Feb 2023)

(d)   Union Minister of State for Home Affairs, Shri Kiren Rijju, Cyber Security-Ministry of Home Affairs, PRESS INFORMATION BUREAU https://pib.gov.in/PressReleaseIframePage.aspx?PRID=1556474 ?(Last Visited 06 Feb 2023)

(e) Extraordinary Gazette of India CG-DL-E-25022021-225464 dated 25 Feb 2021, Ministry of Information and Broadcasting https://mib.gov.in/sites/default/files/Digital%20Media%20Ethics%20Code%20Rules%20%20Notification%20%281%29.pdf (Last visited on 06 Feb 2023)

(f) The Digital Personal Data Protection Act, 2023(Act 22 of 2023)

(g) Information Technology (Intermediary Guidelines and Digital Media Ethics Code) Rules, 2021

4. **Case laws cited**

(a) Kharak Singh V. State of U.P AIR1963 SC 1295

(b) Govind Singh V. State of M.P 1975AIR1378, 1975SCR(3)946

(c) People's Union for Civil Liberties v. Union of India AIR 1997SC568

(d) Unique Identification Authority of India andAnr. V. Central Bureau of Investigation Special Leave to Appeal(Crl) No(s.)2524/2014 order dated 24 mar 2014

(e) Justice K.S. Puttaswamy V Union of India (2017)10 SCC 1

(f) Shreya Singhal V UoI (2015)5 SCC 1

(g) People's Union for Civil Liberties v Union of India MA 901/2021in W.P.(Crl) No.199/2013, 2022 Livelaw (SC) 846